women
in the
garden

O

MARY LOU SANELLI

MW00436262

women
in the
garden

poems

MARY LOU SANELLI

PLEASUREBOATSTUDIO

Copyright © 2001

All rights reserved. This book may not be reproduced, in
whole or part, in any form, except by reviewers, without
the written permission of the publisher.

Cover Artwork by Jacqueline Chisick
Design & Composition by Shannon Gentry
Printed in Canada

Published by
Pleasure Boat Studio: A Literary Press
8630 Wardwell Road
Bainbridge Island•WA 98110-1589 USA
Tel/Fax: 888.810.5308
E-mail: pleasboat@aol.com
URL: http://www.pbstudio.com

Library of Congress Card Number:
2001012345
Women in the Garden/Mary Lou Sanelli
ISBN: 1-929355-14-9
First Printing

For all the women & men
in my garden extraordinaire.
Each friendship nurtures & sustains me.
Each has enabled me to grow.

An Introduction

From my home office where I write today, I look out over my garden, a small and private place, a retreat for my screen-weary eyes to rest upon. Overgrown outside its designated borders, yet weeded methodically within them, it's a haven of contrasting qualities that helps me to understand what is going on inside the perimeters of my own life. How much of me there is in these plantings goes without saying. My poems pry me open and arrive me closer to truth, a walk through my garden the first step to getting there.

And yet, I'm relatively new to gardening, to reworking the soil so I choose what grows. Since this passion first grabbed hold of me, my yard has quickly transformed. In the process, I was moved by the way my new awareness of roots, cuttings, annuals and perennials was affecting my work. Soon each person I was compelled to write about appeared to be standing in his or her own garden, so to speak, tilling a corner of the world. These encounters spurred me on and, like mallow, this collection of poems began to take shape, much larger than first expected.

ACKNOWLEDGMENTS

Poems in this collection have previously appeared in:

Room of One's Own: *What Comes Cracking Into Silence /
After Reading A Brochure On Rape / Morning Lesson*

Pontoon #3 (Floating Bridge Press): *Lightning*

Raven Chronicles: *Missing Laura*

Exhibition (Bainbridge Island Arts Commission): *Ilana*

Art Access: *Hiding From A Friend / Visit During Fiddle Tunes /
Pleasure / February Second / The Gardener*

Between the Lines (Edmonds College): *Private Life*

Tidepools (Peninsula College): *Trading the Squash*

Paperboat Press: *Communion*

Womenwise: *Forgiving*

Spindrift: *Helen and Two Toddlers, Emma and Max*

Phoenix Rising Newsletter: *Women in the Garden*

Calapooya Collage: *Keja's Questions*

Womens Work: *What She Misses*

Poets for Habitat for Humanity: *Pleasure*

CONTENTS

"In search of my mother's garden,
I found my own."
—Alice Walker

WOMEN IN THE GARDEN

My neighbor drenches her yard, pumps water
into a garden gone to seed, pitiful
heap of weeds, but I don't think of wastefulness
rather how her white curls lie in stark contrast
to a rosy scalp, visible through her hair
as a wound, pink as a tropical morning
and how spraying mist from an uncoiled hose
lends serenity to her whole, smooth face.

When I look up into the limbs of a tree
it's difficult to distinguish a single leaf. One
merely blends with the contours of another
much like my life entwines with other women's lives
so I will know how to take my place
in the arms of the future.

I'm wondering about the woman
next door again, what wills her to care
for dullness, for flowers collapsed and faded, unfit
for vases while I rush to the nursery to buy
what blooms erect and high-priced. How easy.
How short lived.

When she opens another umbrella
of wetness, the shower extends to my garden
waving its playful color. Her body leans forward
into the flow, as if she longs to follow
each silver droplet
winding its way to the renewal of sea.

Each day, she is so tiny
an aperture I peer into to see
clear through to the end, the quieting down
that is promised when we release like reins
the task that holds us in mother-sized arms
to earth, unrelenting as the memory
of what our life was.

THIS OTHER WAY

Her sink. Her guests. Her china
engraved with green-and-white wreaths
swirling each rounded edge. Her son
staring, face set with aching
tenderness he doesn't yet know he bestows
on a woman like me, childless
by choice, but still...

When a door is opened to air the sun-baked kitchen,
herbs growing on the sill sway in the air
sweeping cool over a room that clicks
with the sound of plates. The boy touches a few
delicate leaves, says aloud what he has learned to name:
basil, thyme, sweet william. His mother, busy
twisting heads of lettuce till each heart pulls
from its core, doesn't pause to acknowledge
so he repeats what he sees: *basil, thyme, sweet william,*
looking to me for praise, causing my own center to lift
from its hold and linger

while I try on this other way of washing dishes
as a hostess, wife, homeowner, mother—
hands pressed into soapy water, teaching a child
to name what grows, repeating the words
ten or twenty times a sink load.
Whatever it takes.

MISSING LAURA

When Laura collapsed by the compost,
she was tossing chard on the heap, huge
excesses of pulpy green. I like to think without pain
or warning, her body merely paused, then slid
onto rain-moistened earth, a faint sigh
echoing the stillness like laughter
traveling over spacious land.

Laura knew how to talk to local men
who work in the woods as well as to the swarthy one
from New York who deals blackjack in the casino
rising like a strip mall on the edge of town,
parking lots surrounding it
broad as the wealth inside. Farmland,
Laura reminded him, that last year was a field of poppies
bolting red, but she liked his east coast candor
when he looked her square in the eyes and said, *Christ,*
a job's a job when you owe three month's rent.

I'll never forget how cold she was
like skimming my fingers over ice, or her stillness
awkward in my arms. At first, I thought she slept,
abandoning us for a little quiet, but no shudder
of living rustled when I called then yelled her name.
That's when I screamed and the others came running.
Not one of us knew what to do except look down

in disbelief. The world, suddenly, too over-exposed
to see, too piercing to hear.

Now, in the absence of light
I press my body to my husband's back,
lie motionless, eyes open
and afraid of the deepening night.
This is when he whispers *it's true*
tragic things occur, but we have each other,
our life is good…adding hope to my thoughts
consumed by an image of my world falling away
one Laura at a time.

WHAT COMES CRACKING
INTO SILENCE

Asleep, I'm a girl again, nipples humming
in the backseat of my boyfriend's car
sunk deep in a cul-de-sac
like a submarine ready to sneak away
if enemy beacons (my father's headlights) creep up
through the steamy dark where we lie
unashamed, arousal rushing our brains
with the wine we swig, bodies stacked, legs waving
midair like laundry in the wind. Through our jeans
we grind away, fumble for another hit
of pleasure under a layer of breath
dangling above our heads transparent as gauze.

Then, as if beads of sweat,
the impassioned scene ripples away
indifferently, as morning splashes up in waves
over the room. What I want to do is fall
back into that dream of denim sex and pretend
to things younger, to suck on the past like caramel.
But I hoist myself up, shake off
reminiscence, untie the laces of memory
and ease into wanting what is
true and rising from a place
inside a deeper place. Yet, even as I do
the work and remember to focus,
I hear it grazing the silence, youth
tearing up like sheets
of ice on a March pond.

LIGHTNING

When doctors use the word *attack*
again and again, she winces, wants
another term for what befalls a heart
that right up to the end
beat with kindness. Hearts like her husband's
are *not* attacked. They simply stop.
The giving complete.

She found him lying by the trellis
where hollyhocks grow tall as young trees.
On his hands, the leather gloves she wrapped
for Christmas with a book on bonsai.
He wanted to try it, caring for a maze
of intricate roots, to clip each hair-like strand
by instinct.

The next step is to telephone friends
more like family than any family she knows.
Then a walk on the path at the edge of town
where she pauses at a charred tree stump
with its roots exposed, perched on the sand
like an excavation. *This is what it's like,*
she thinks, *lightning has struck*
and only part of me is left.

THE NEST

When I step outside
into autumn's crisp arrival,
I remember bulbs I replanted,
unearthing a fist full into the spreading light
to share a few with Sheila who said
she'd never noticed such striking bluebells.

That's what we call them, *bluebells,*
though on a picnic last July
Sheila got drunk and declared them blue*balls.*
Mad at men more than renaming a flower, we laughed
into evening, two hearts big on the blanket and Sheila
just got drunker because she dreaded going home
to bicker, her husband's will hulked in the corner
like a prize fighter.

So I stay on my back looking up,
not taking the indistinct mound for a nest
bunched tightly overhead until I climb up
to probe what seems a part of me
missing and sure enough, as I lift
the mass from its hold, my own hair
spills feathers, falls to the palm of my hand.
And before I know what I've ruined, a finch,
in a flurry of wingbeats, bolts
from its summer glove.

THE GIRL IN THE WINDOW

This year I ease into fall
with a strong desire for change, shed summer
easily, dragging a hose through the yard, pacing
under an August sun to keep my acre green.
Now, water releases itself in fog, rain,
each cleansing dew. Perennials draw back. Sleep.
A few annuals hang on, pale versions of spring selves.
Dandelions spread unchecked,
irrespective of how many times
I dug their roots on my knees. Tired of the garden,
I work inside, put up jars of herb vinegar, sugar pickles,
jam. When my spoon clinks the glass again
and again I think of the tone as a rhythm
of doing, a sound that pleasures my solitude.

By dusk, chores make their way
to the outside where the world around me
opens, is mine for the having. I love the blush
twilight makes, soft but steadfast, making ready for nightfall
as I rake and stack kindling. The air shivers cool
without sound reminding me of the girl
framed in a dormer last night, her eyes like wounds
unable to heal as I strolled a neighborhood appearing safe
and privileged from the street.

Then shouting pierced the calm, brutal
as sirens at dawn and I feared the house
like one fears a handgun, the dark barrel.
A man's accusations. A woman's
plunging equally cruel. In the upstairs window
a girl cupping her ears. Above, a star-lavish sky.
I searched for one just letting go. I wanted to
make a wish for her, to think of something useful,
merciful, complete to say. I walked on
knowing I would find no words
adequate to manage so much.

TRADING THE SQUASH

I pry apart broad, prickly leaves
to find a pair of tiny pumpkins
shiny as knickknacks
making dull the weeds surrounding them and the land
I kneel before as if to kiss or take a sip.
To observe my raised bed spill open
with orange-yellow light, I can imagine
my crop in a cornucopia, each fruit
a star.

When I visit a master of this knowledge
of growing, whose garden is mother-wise
to my newborn patch of soil, I share my yield
and she returns the gesture, hers pruned
from a greenhouse where green tomatoes hang
in hopes of ripening to a shade
somewhat closer to red. This trading moves me
happily, my body fills with satisfaction that nearly quakes
out loud, but I don't mention it. It simply collects
like recycling, has weight, takes up space,
and lingers late into the week.

I learn in modest increments. About gardens.
About whatever drapes my life
and fits: small offerings with sea
in clear view, crows riding the wind, autumn sun
resembling summer's, the belly of a yard
in full presence and bloom.

LATER THE SAME DAY

When one has sat alone for hours
writing at a desk surrounded by windows
so all of life's movement is visible
but elsewhere, it is necessary to surrender
to spring's green warmth, to a yard
swelling with firm new buds.
Outside, skirt hiked up, my pale legs
exposed like rooftops to the sun, I'm content
to watch a robin peck at compost
for fine threads of nest-weed, her fullness
round as a peach.

Later, when I drive to the airport
to meet my exchange student,
you cannot imagine how little we find
to say to each other. Her face is stunning
as her figure and her insistent lack of luggage
punctuates our separateness... when I travel,
so much of me trails behind. All the way home,
I long to return to the rhythm of a yard I created
with my hands and faith. How can this girl be so lovely...
I feel awkward, body dangling, unsure of its place.
What happened to the morning's simplicity
of bird song, its soothing effect? Now, harsher
sounds of passage wallow in my ears, an absence
of solace filling the farthest reach
between my ribs.

Once home, I escape
to the toolshed, close my eyes and try
to let go, to shift my thoughts forward and back
in step with things whole and satisfying.
And in the solitude that makes my existence
worthwhile, I'm able to hold
to the present, to what my life is.

COMMUNION

Jesse visits with my birthday
in a lunch bag, canned pears
she knows I cherish because last week
at her place she served them and later
watched me gulp the rest from the jar.
To share fruit put up so impeccably as this
is communion.

But more than a syrupy offering
I pick up and place
gratefully down, its her bestowal of time.
Our bodies relax, no push–pull
as we speak, hungry
to know how far words
will equally take us.

Tomorrow we must work, rush
past each other with a smile and brush
of hand, busy with varied selves
craving sun, less wind
as much as anything as winter nights pass
under a skyline
free of city lights, by day
shielding us from the blue
a sky gives.

PILGRIMAGE

When the sharp edge of a window box
catches my temple, a snap
of pain hurtles me to the ground. Lately,
many movements send me
spinning like this, separate my body
abruptly from intention.

The way I see it
one of two women has returned, one
no less cagey than the other, to remind me
coincidence occurs when the subconscious aches
to be received. When its message
craves to be heard until realized
inside itself.

Either Loretta has transported her will
from all directions like mint
in my lavender bed, to inform me it makes her
nervous
all the changes springing up like decoys
under my roof, impeding her memories
of a previous life in my home. Or the daughter
I desire and at the same time
do not, has decided to apply herself
to my body like a scratchy dressing, intruding
by aggressive means. How like me she is!

I fear if my resistance endures, she will continue

to reveal herself, swirling into mind
midpoint between menstruations
so as not to miss a monthly pilgrimage
only we concede until the day I let her slide
away like a doily from the arm of a chair
or summon her to enter
this world by way of me.

VISITING JENN

I need to stand and walk away
from my desk, drive miles out of town
to peel the pace of my life back so I will forget
what it is I'm supposed to do next. Too long
alone with words, the keys of my computer click
like worry beads under my fingers.

When I navigate the path through woods
and weeds brushing my car
toward a bright space in all the other space
where her home is built
and beyond, the sea opening to more,
I thought this *is* Jenn because personality
of place molds us more deeply than will
or any part of our past.

When I knock, wind chimes lend a jingling
to the air seductive as music, the smooth grooves
meant to make love by. Though my friend isn't home,
I walk her yard, hold her cat
as if a baby in my arms, fondle my toes
in soil, lose myself like pollen in wind.
By the garden, a rake and hoe lean like lovers
backed into the fence for a kiss. Such is the power
of contentment.

I mix lettuce and kale, eat
from the palm of my hand, swallow whole

the fact of this day: everything right, nothing
missing. Belonging. Gratitude
sprawled across my breasts
like a newborn. No self
scrutiny under sunlight or later...
the stars.

HIDING FROM A FRIEND

Patience *is* a virtue
but this morning, annoyance is all I manage
to summon before work can begin.
The week's dishes stacked in the sink
are not the least of my worries as the phone rings
and rings, pushing through any claims
to quiet. And when my friend pulls up
in front of the house, unsuspecting
of my frustration by now big as the power
pole rising imposingly beside her car,
she walks my yard with a gift
of generosity that makes me want to serve up tea
and sit. But I yearn to write and there is a spark
of panic as I run to the bathroom, drop to all fours
and go silent. Breathing slows, heart quickens.
Blood rushes to my face. Reflection in the glass
is of a woman crouching in her own home
as if an air raid blares overhead.

Later my friend tells me she knew I was inside
because something about the stillness
tightened around her like a noose
instead of welcoming her like a bed
of grass and flowers will when void
of people and noise.
The poet in me feels justified
though I apologize just the same,
making another moment between us

to store away like a nosegay
though more like something seeded
in love than such a dry
and crumbly remembrance.

ILANA

Last summer she returned home
when an uncle died. Three years prior,
her sister, in the throes of divorce, pleaded
she find her way back. But typically, no contact
with parents in New Jersey
with little interest in a daughter who takes yoga
seriously and lives on an ocean
they've never seen. Time comes between people.
Love is reluctant. It can come to nothing.

We both know what it's like to choose life
with no buzzing of children.
Know what's expected of our bodies
is nonexistent and doesn't move us
toward a place that temporarily takes the place
of what it is we still need to do next.

Stepping outside, we hear the screen door
snap behind us, rousing an array of cats
appearing here and there on the grass.
I notice how plump they are like felines
in a Max Grover painting, though when I say so
I regret it instantly, try to absolve my blunder
by praising her lilies, spiky pedals of white
waving sturdy under a tentative sky
of shifting blue we agree tears us down
in winter and rain. When I trust her
with another confidence, from the corner

of my eye, I watch her hold back,
know at this moment we will not be friends,
unlike when, younger and hesitant to trust myself,
I'd return to her, wanting something other than what is
inevitable, embarking on a quest
to be liked, wondering if gut instinct
that shakes my body in its hands
reliably exists.

GREEN TOMATOES

The falling sun drags shadows
across my hollyhocks
sagging leisurely into scarlet runners
ascending toward a flimsy spire
where five stakes meet.

The first thing my friend says
as she walks my yard is that I plant *too much,* insists
without compassion my vegetation is choking.
For the rest of the day, her opinion of my garden
turning on itself makes me curse
her precise beds, erect and studied as ballerinas
who haven't a clue how to dance to Motown.

My hands are my mother's, the same fan-shaped nails
and transparent skin revealing a crosshatch of blue.
Yet, my father's need to dig into soil
and make salads grow is what I renew
each short warm season
watching my single row of blight-ridden,
rain-mildewed tomatoes result in a harvest
I hold in one hand.

Lately, when I wear yellow-lens sunglasses
because my neighbor swears they ward off winter
depression, I imagine each green fruit bolting
fully ripe and sweet, color so deep-seated
it nears black where stems rise out of pulp

ample enough to puree. My whole childhood held
in the shade and smell of pasta sauce
boiling in ball jars, smudging my chin, staining
my young life red.

VISIT DURING FIDDLE TUNES

for Margo

Once a year she visits in bright, fertile June
after the last rhododendron blooms
wriggle free and buckle on the lawn.
My challenge is to fix lunch
in time allotted between her music workshops
taught in a state park near my home.

This summer I mix pasta with garlic
sautéed in soy, olive oil, a fist of fresh herbs.
As she serves herself, I'm greedy for more
conversation, grow anxious
watching the clock.

Today, clear sky, sun
rising to the highest peak without a single cloud
screening its light. Still, it is not enough
to slow an hour wedged between the rest of the day
and our bond. My mouth releases more
of what is on my mind
even as she walks from my yard,
bends her body into a car, turns
the wheel and drives away
so slowly it leaves me wanting
to run alongside foolishly waving.
The idea lingers, resists, passes
as I stoop to pick up a few cedar sprays
where spring winds tossed
them whole onto the grass.

AFTER READING A BROCHURE ON RAPE

What statistics say about crimes against women,
how frequently they occur, suffering
you cannot imagine... leveled me
in one quick sweep, compressed
my lungs, backed into me like a dumptruck
splaying fear like a ton of brick. I try to summon
the confidence I felt moments ago
before eyeing the brochure. If my mother were here
she would say *it doesn't happen to good girls...*
and we would argue till I remember she lives
in a smaller sphere than the world I know.
It's a phenomenon how a closed mind works,
how it pushes away *opening* by reflex,
as if knowledge were flames
advancing hotter and hotter...but all I want to ponder
today is how do I protect myself knowing each minute
is the one before another gun goes off?

Let the sky tell its story, stars sink
and scatter, seasons roll over my green plot of land
at no burden to me, but this wedge of reality
leaves a sinkhole. I stumble. Fall. The lights go out.
Dread glows in the dark as if the white
part of my eye, circles my life
with gravestones.

It would please me no end
to pass this truth on like clothes I'm tired of.
Instead of the spontaneous woman I was,
I've grown cautious, bravado vanished
as if water down a drain. I wash my hands
of trust which runs against my nature, saddens me
until I see a man in the stairwell, grinning
without mercy as he slams his body into mine.
Coyotes savaging my cat to pieces, her limbs
torn free, organs devoured reminding me
nature *is* cruel, is made up of and is measured by
its cruelness.

MORNING LESSON

When I read poetry in the morning
my own lines creep up like chickweed
through the day, notes by the phone, bed,
on a pad suction-cupped to the windshield
of my car. A catchy tune is what it's like,
uttering itself over and over till I stomp my foot
or whine in frustration, but still
words keep coming.

Even in precious summer, say mid-July,
scent of a dryer musking the yard in domesticity,
Seattle on sabbatical, excusing itself
briefly from familiarity of gray, a quick thrill
like a sneeze before rain returns. The kind of day
I want outsideness to fill me, yet the comfort of work
favors my office. Here is where I know
what I really think.

Whereas, begin my day
thumbing through a clothes catalogue
and nowhere, no way, do the women within
remind me of me. Women like sparklers, skinny
displays of pageantry till I'm left
with *my* nakedness which, suddenly, I've seen
enough of to last me. I'll drop to my knees
like Aunt Connie in her garden and give thanks
when thirty- to eighty-year-old women
at home in real bodies fill the pages of ads.

Best selves basking in grace. Dignity.
Pride. All of that and nothing
we fear about ourselves
their courage can't uproot.

WHAT IT'S LIKE

My friend with no use of her legs
wants to know what it's like to walk
on ones muscled and shapely
as an athlete's, to kick
someone and swiftly run away.

To hike until so fatigued she trips
over two strained feet.

To wrap more than arms
around a man and press into him
till all their limbs wind
like ribbons round one another.

My friend asks me to know
her way of moving when we sit
out back on a slab of blacktop,
torches of scotch broom flaring
yellow against sky and heat
rising from the dewy surface
like steam from a mug of tea.
Clumsy with awkwardness, I climb
onto her lap and roll with her
in a canvas chair, wheels leaving
thin tracks, a translucent wake
as I share the ease of movement
promised.

When we stop, I lurch forward, fall
into my leg-sturdy world I want restored
regardless of a smile
beaming from inside my head and all
I painstakingly say, surprised
how little self-consciousness it takes
to undo me.

FORGIVING

Every so often you rush
into memory. Who knows why?
A particular curve
to a cheekbone, a stranger's mouth
droops slack, too heavy to close...
and your face floods in.

I can manage, though, keep you
from splashing the rest of my life
the way you used to in raging waves,
you could say I lived my life back then
soaking wet. Now, I'm able to balance
the remembering
no hands while riding a bicycle
without spilling a drop.

I can do this, quiet myself
through a string of winters
till cold backs off, the air appeased
with warmth, the effort
of forgiveness no longer so huge
it pins me to the floor. Instead, something
softer like twilight, a rosebush
thriving between house and fence.
Even with their impossibilities: dusk
as luminous everyday, stems
aging thornless, smooth
as petals above.

I DID NOT INVEST IN MICROSOFT

but in a cottage-sized home, unpretentious
as the flimsy trellis it hides behind
where clematis spills open under five cedar trees.
In spring, when we rake up the windfalls,
a dozen new mole hills rise up, skillfully
torn from a weed-infiltrated lawn.

As advised, I've amassed a portfolio:
A thousand shares of marriage, bonds
to friendship with a lien against those
lost to AIDS, cancer, a car wreck on Sims Way.
Or the worst unraveling, one meaningless skirmish
shattering years of trust as we live on
though separately, the distance between us
tense as harp strings. When I take stock
of my life, I want each camaraderie restored
with cinematic tears, hugs, forgiveness
regardless of the effort it takes.

All afternoon and here I am still
writing these words that shine
like steel gadgets shine, bright as sun
on snow or computer screens in every night
office on Seattle's east side.

Come fall, I increase my savings
of lavender from a bush where bees

hum in the air, the sound
soft as the moss at my feet. Merger of knife
to stem, an enterprise making millions
of purplish seeds. A contract
between a fragrant shrub and me, the reward
nearly solid, real as what I cut and hold.

TERESA TALKS AND I REMEMBER

And so it is the season of my life
when the young become wiser
and through them I'm delivered to a place
inside myself withdrawn
like ink lines left in sun, a potted plant
unwatered too long, diminished
but waiting.

I don't remember when I started drinking coffee
but I remember Teresa serving a cup
one dreary January day, tourists gone, locals left
to reclaim a rain-worn, dreary downtown.
A particular style to her pleasantries
magnified by the fact she looked me square
in the eye with confidence airy around her,
visible as steam.

Today, sitting in my garden,
she tells me the key to joy is friendship, words
still glowing in her chair
way after she stands and walks off
leaving my past stirring...

  before men and marriage
  before career and mortgage
  before life lifted a part of me
  like a thief

and I think back
to when my friends and I took time
for whole pots of tea to trickle through our lips
and still we stayed
stuck to these same lawn chairs
clasping our mugs, bodies bent forward
as we took one more turn
to make something complete
from what lacked in us each.

KEJA'S QUESTIONS

flow naturally as singing.
A six-year-old stream of thought
not yet sandbagged in places.

I pay her to pick camellia bouquets,
lavish pink clusters in bulk. I watch
her strut outside, high-heeled, prickly-blue tutu
round her waist as she turns into her girlself,
concealed till recently, but primed
like painted fingernails curled in a fist.

Bored with the task of pleasing, she explodes
into my office. I'm writing so I don't look up.
Her will waits the briefest snip of a moment
then stomps its foot in the middle of the room.
Her fervor, like the moon we see by at night
as if it were day, reminds me of me, is a sentence
I can read. I search for a word
lush enough to make my fondness whole.
Her quiz helps shape my tongue that falters, pauses
before rising to the bait: *Where will you go*
when you die? Will bugs eat you and wild dogs
dig your stinky butt up? Do you and Larry, you know,
sex together? She is fearless. *Now,* she says,
kiss me like a boy. So I do.

My affection for her is lacy-red and smooth
as a negligee. Love like this grounds me
to an impossible body as if the weight
inside my chest is a delicate bird
thrashing the ribs of its cage.

FEBRUARY SECOND

for Rachel

All morning, rain and wind.
Trees lean and spread like awnings
over the water-soaked ground, the one-lane streets.
I rake lopped branches into a pile, the pile into the compost

before calling the hospital to check on my friend
in labor since dawn. I imagine her bracing
each assault of pain with a thin white pillow
propped between her knees. And grasping
her husband's hand, the nurse's, her own
clenched prayer-like, binding two limbs
for strength.

No one answers the phone in maternity
and I think of driving there but it is too far
a leap into another's privacy so I busy off
to the bank, post office, grocery. Distract
my concern piercing the day like sun breaks falling
long across the road. When I look up
at the startling glimpse of blue, I am helpless

yet confident tender care will be given
my friend as a son pours his life around her.
And when she cradles him, she will feel his fingers,
each splendid toe, her separate self
for the last time. His fragrant body
as much a part of her arms now
as the elbow or wrist, the silent blue web
of veins beneath, incapable of rest.

PRIVATE LIFE

I plant a package of tulip bulbs
wrist deep in compost, steam
rising as I work the humid heap.
Beneath my trowel
the earth simmers. Heat comes even
from the top tier of loam.

The idea of crocus
displaying the world at my feet
eases the onset of winter
months I find difficult to embrace,
easier to encircle
with irises, daffodils
enough to wind the yard, narcissus
I failed to plant adequately deep
so delicate shoots emerge
lopsided, cockeyed
blooms of linen white.

I've learned to gauge
how many it takes, one
not too near the other.
My palm surrounds the dormant clump,

crisp sheaths falling away in bits
like confetti when I open my hand.
A pause
like prayer without moving
my lips. Then the burying

one by one...

days grow shorter.

HELEN AND TWO TODDLERS, EMMA AND MAX

When the season starts to darken in late August,
the light changes to an orangey blush that falls
across a toy-strewn room and a velvet armchair
the muted color of muscle, the lush human heart.
This is where I curl into the blaze of softness
and wait to catch a ride with Helen.

A row of poplars gives way to gladiolus
still standing this dry summer day
and then we pile into the jeep, Helen, Emma, and Max
slipping into the back. I'm in the front
and all the way to the city I think it takes
a patient woman to read to a little girl
while a boy twitches and tests her nerves,
sun beats through glass, clothes grow prickly
as crinolines, knees are crammed,
and a son's protests are shrill bursts
into muggy air.

Now the boy gives in
to drowsiness, body slanted, head bobbing each stop
and go. The rest of the ride is quiet save for Helen
still reading to Emma, everything I'd want in a daughter
if I could rouse myself to go through with it. Lately
I trade places with women like Helen
momentarily in mind, or longer

when mother-ness surrounds my senses
like a lei of orchids, inoculating me
briefly
from the life I know.

PLEASURE

Slicing tomatoes and basil I stand
at the sill admiring a yard
freshly weeded, each crisp shoot
snapped free of its root
so I fool myself into believing
there is perfection in the world.

My husband kisses the back of my neck.
I continue cutting. Chives, a clove of garlic.
The house is quiet. I cook
but the house is quiet.

Not enough beans. Outside,
coolness sudden to my feet, I pick from vines
ascending bamboo stakes that lean
into an axis, the symmetry
where three poles cross.
I find most things in life
as chancy. Getting narrowly by
under a makeshift cover.

And then a sunset, the violet air
detailing the madrone, its peeling-red bark.
An abundance of fresh food
so we are ushered to the brink
of pleasure, compelled
to ease a need to busy ourselves, to know
and receive the multitude of splendor
that makes up our living till our hearts come round
fully awakened.

NEW ORLEANS

In my hotel room I sit
looking down on the French Quarter,
its red doors, geraniums, chimneys
and hues to the streets where the Mississippi floods
with mud the color of brick.

Not forgetting what happened here
happened, I'm sorry
slaves sold for a dollar in Jackson Square,
for our deplorable history and the way I am
out of my element in the deep south. But tonight
I lay my white guilt down
along with a Northwest way of dressing
for comfort and cold, to dance
in sleazy heels and a short, black dress
on Bourbon Street at the 544 Club
to soulful music that pulls me from the grasp
of a slower way of life in a small town so safe
in comparison to this southern city
where homes display alarm warnings
like huge, proper wreaths,
separating those with so much to lose
from the ones who look on
from tenements five minutes away.

Driving a highway headed north, magnolia trees
hovering above, a great white plantation house
poses cathedral-like, just as godly

in the center of a soft green lawn, and I think
it is possible to look deeply into a landscape's eyes
like a con man's and see
only lies.

WHAT SHE MISSES

A gardenia-scented bath. A rinse
for her hair from sprigs of rosemary
picked fresh, just this morning.
Weeding the garden on her knees
in a flannel shirt. Her body
full of want
instead of exhaustion, her mood
sucked dry by work, work
she knows she needs
because to not have it
exhausts her more
and worse, makes her afraid
because she's been there
wondering where the money will come from
but more than that, wondering
who she is and what she will do
for herself. Her family.
Self-esteem going right out the door
with the dog. So this work
she complains about is not so bad she says
she needs to complain is all
because she misses life,
sex, camaraderie,
the way it used to be
spontaneous before the mortgage, car,
kids.

OPENING THE DOOR

I want you to have it, no
I demand you take it back, the shame
you left me, holding fast as shadows
when the sun is low.

Until now. Just look at me,
at the light raining in.
And I laugh again.
And trust.

I am not forgiving you. That is more
than I can dress-up and pretend.
I'm just ready to move into spring
after a season so long and cold,
one hundred winters back to back.

I think of this passage
as walking through an open door
to the green house.
Strong magnificent earthy scent.
And when I clear away
leaves and moss, there they be
a lot like my unfolding, perennials
with roots and buds
in want of so much.

THE GARDENER

for Greg

I walk up to a three-story home of stucco,
a great grey pose poised in sunlight
winter-low in the sky. Beyond, the rising earth
of islands: Whidbey. San Juan. Ebey's Landing,
the lowest point across the sound.
Yesterday's wind and rain whirled away,
leaving this yard hushed and steaming:
a four-square garden pruned just so
bordered by a sprawl of what grows
without care.

He tells me he lives completely
accepted for the man he is. His voice
draws me in, no holding back
and silencing what it is still left to say.
The rest of our conversation... easy mostly,
a few pauses. When he remembers pulling weeds
to buy his first car, we launch
through the lull. Nothing spiritual
happens, he says, when he burrows into soil.
What he seeks is transition
of space, leaning a cedar-fringed landscape
toward the oriental. Japanese Maples.
Pagoda Trees. And there are things
he does not speak openly about, though
he does not keep hidden

when he hikes with his father into the hills
or by some river rolling them along. No need
to hold his life up to the light
in the face of his father's love that is generous
as the very things between men they do know
how to share.

Other books from
Pleasure Boat Studio: A Literary Press

Fiction

Another Life and Other Stories, by Edwin Weihe
If You Were With Me Everything Would Be All Right,
stories by Ken Harvey
In Memory of Hawks, and Other Stories from Alaska,
by Irving Warner
Pronoun Music, stories by Richard Cohen
Setting Out: The Education of Li-li, a novel by Tung Nien,
translated from the Chinese by Mike O'Connor
The Eighth Day of the Week, a novel by Alfred Kessler

Poetry

In Blue Mountain Dusk, by Tim McNulty. A Broken Moon book
Lineage, by Mary Lou Sanelli. An Empty Bowl book
Nature Lovers, by Charles Potts
Original Sin, by Michael Daley. Chapbook
P'u Ming's Oxherding Tales, by P'u Ming, translated from the
Chinese by Red Pine. An Empty Bowl book
Saying the Necessary, by Edward Harkness
The Basin: Life in a Chinese Province,
by Mike O'Connor. An Empty Bowl book
The Light on Our Faces: A Therapy Dialogue,
by Lee Miriam Whitman-Raymond. Chapbook
The Politics of My Heart, by William Slaughter
The Rainshadow, by Mike O'Connor. An Empty Bowl book
The Rape Poems, by Frances Driscoll
The Straits, by Michael Daley. An Empty Bowl book
Too Small to Hold You, by Kate Reavey. Chapbook
Untold Stories, by William Slaughter. An Empty Bowl book

Essays

The Handful of Seeds: Three and a Half Essays,
by Andrew Schelling. Chapbook
When History Enters the House: Essays from Central Europe,
by Michael Blumenthal

Pleasure Boat Studio: A Literary Press
8630 Wardwell Road
Bainbridge Island•WA 98110-1589 USA
Tel/Fax: 888.810.5308
URL: www.pbstudio.com

from
Pleasure Boat Studio

an essay written by Ouyang Xiu,
Song Dynasty poet, essayist, and scholar,
on the twelfth day of the twelfth month
in the **renwu** year (January 25, 1043)

I have heard of men of antiquity who fled from
the world to distant rivers and lakes and
refused to their dying day to return. They
must have found some source of pleasure
there. If one is not anxious for profit, even at
the risk of danger, or is not convicted of a
crime and forced to embark; rather, if one has
a favorable breeze and gentle seas and is
able to rest comfortably on a pillow and mat,
sailing several hundred miles in a single day,
then is boat travel not enjoyable? Of course, I
have no time for such diversions. But since
'pleasure boat' is the designation of boats
used for such pastimes, I have now adopted it
as the name of my studio. Is there anything
wrong with that?

Translated by Ronald Egan
The Literary Works of Ou-yang Hsiu
Cambridge University Press

Photo by Maxine Lewis Seran

About the Author

Mary Lou Sanelli was raised in Connecticut, edu-
cated in Boston, and now lives and works in
Port Townsend, a small coastal town located on
Washington state's Olympic Peninsula, and in Seattle's
vibrant downtown Belltown district. Sanelli's previous
collections include *Close At Hand* (High Plains Press),
Long Steaks of Flashing Daylight (Blue Begonia Press),
and *Lineage* (Empty Bowl Press). Her poems have also
been published widely in journals and anthologies
including *The Seattle Review, Calyx, Crab Creek Re-
view, Pontoon* (Floating Bridge Press), and others. Her
work will appear in *Woven on the Wind: A Collection of
Western Women Writers* (Houghton Mifflin, 2001). She
coordinates Port Townsend's celebrated *Sunday at One
Poetry Series,* now in its fifteenth year, and she is Artis-
tic Director of **The Moving Arts Dance Company.**